Ann,

Many thanks from your colleagues at Washington & Lee.

By George!

By George!

MR. WASHINGTON'S GUIDE TO CIVILITY TODAY

Steven Michael Selzer

**Andrews McMeel
Publishing**

Kansas City

05 06 07 08 09 RDC 10 9 8 7 6 5 4 3 2

Library of Congress Cataloging-in-Publication Data
Washington, George, 1732-1799.
    By George! : Mr. Washington's guide to civility today / George Washington and Steven Michael Selzer.
        p.   cm.
    ISBN 0-7407-0610-1
        1. Washington, George, 1732-1799—Philosophy. 2. Etiquette.
    I. Selzer, Steven Michael. II. Title.
    E312.78 2000
    973.4'1'092—dc21   99-87574

Book designed and typeset by Susan Hood Design.

---

*In memory of Nathan Selzer, my father, and
Walter Heafitz, father of my very civil wife, Adrianne*

ACKNOWLEDGMENTS

Few books result from the efforts of one person. This one is no exception. I owe thanks to many, beginning with my wife, who is my model of civility. Adrianne is always other-directed and empathetic, selfless and kind, tactful and caring. Her kind parents, Walter and Betty Heafitz, are fine examples of my theory that civil behavior begins at home. My parents, Nathan and Florence, and my sister, Karen Leopold, can also be counted among the very civil. I am most grateful to my family for the example they set as I was growing up and to my sons, Ethan and Elliott, for their support.

Among the many teachers who played an important role in my life, none compares to Joe Black, the former Brooklyn Dodgers pitcher who was my teacher and mentor. His counsel and civil behavior are both exemplary.

Alan Sultan helped inspire and advise me, as did Maggie Bedrosian. Jody Rein's initial enthusiasm has not waned. She is a truly skilled and civil literary agent. The editing of Alice Levine and Ginny Golder-Magid has been of great importance. The constructive criticism of the manuscript by my sister, Karen, was of key significance.

I would like to acknowledge the voluntary participation of the following people in a civility focus group I organized: Michael Banks, Maggie Bedrosian, Cynthia Foster, Randy Mayer, Alan Sultan, and Alexandra Titus.

My alma mater, The George Washington University, has been very supportive. The university was founded in 1821 due to a bequest left by our Founding Father. It proudly bears his name in the nation's capital. I would particularly like to thank Dr. Laura Violand, Assistant Vice President Sandy Holland, Barbara Porter, Dr. Kathryn Napper, Dr. Walter Bortz, Vice President Robert Chernak, and President Stephen Trachtenberg.

My paralegal, Joan Canterbury, has assisted me in many ways, which include allowing me to tap into her excellent judgment. Drs. Michael Manyak and Steven Patierno, both associated with George Washington University, are performing important cancer research. A portion of the royalties from *By George!* will be contributed to this cause. It's wonderful feeling to be a small participant in the battle against cancer, and I thank the purchasers of this book for making it possible.

Finally, I would like to acknowledge my publisher for

---

embracing this topic. Patty Rice, senior editor, has been particularly enthusiastic; her passionate approach to the subject helped *By George!* find a welcoming home. Jennifer Fox has been a pleasure to work with. I am proud that the team at Andrews McMeel saw fit to publish this book.

INTRODUCTION

Rudeness. Crudeness. Thoughtlessness. Uncivilized behavior is everywhere. From the boss who publicly chews out her assistant, to the driver who barrels dangerously down the highway, to the sports fan who yells obscenities at the ball game, there is little doubt that we live in an increasingly barbaric world. And it's just as clear that many of us would like to see things change.

Polls indicate that a great many Americans long for greater civility because the way we treat one another has a powerful impact on our daily life. Civility in this context goes beyond good manners. It means behaving honorably and ethically in all aspects of our lives.

The problem is we just don't know how to behave anymore. On the one hand we're taught to be forthright and assertive in our interactions, while on the other hand there is an expectation that we will be extremely polite—even passive—when faced with a problem or conflict. The mixed messages are confusing and misleading. What

Americans need is a model of civility, one we can look to for insight and inspiration.

Sometimes, in order to move forward, we need to take a long look back. Enter George Washington. Washington was a person of great integrity who remains one of the most revered figures in the history of our country. The youngest schoolchildren know George Washington could not tell a lie. But what is far less commonly known is that at the age of fourteen the father of our country jotted down 110 rules of civility and decent behavior.

Washington carried that list of guidelines with him throughout his life. Although they were written more than 250 years ago, they remain pertinent and valuable.*

In this book, as these wonderful old rules are brought to bear on modern problems and sticky social situations, it becomes clear just how important the way we treat each other affects us all. Although being "civilized" has a quaint, out-of-date ring, it is by no means out of fashion. More and more people crave its return. The incidents abound. In 1999, for example, a sheriff's deputy invoked a hundred-year-old Michigan law when he ticketed a

---

* Two notes about the language of these rules. First, some of the more archaic words of Washington's rules have been "translated" to their modern equivalents for ease of understanding. These changes are shown in brackets. Second, in Washington's time all reference to gender was in the masculine. A change to modern practice would have robbed the original of its authenticity, so this language has been retained.

man for swearing loudly for several minutes within earshot of children. The cultural ramifications of the way we treat one another in private and in public have never been more poignant than they are today. The headlines in every daily paper speak volumes. We seek concrete answers. George Washington can help us find them.

The Rules

EVERY ACTION DONE IN COMPANY OUGHT TO BE DONE WITH SOME SIGN OF RESPECT TO THOSE THAT ARE PRESENT.

Everybody wants and deserves respect. But it seems to be in short supply these days. Some people say they don't get any; and Aretha Franklin says just a little bit will do. It's up to all of us to increase the world's supply of respect. As you go through your day, consider all the people you come in contact with, from the paper deliverer to your boss to the body-pierced teenager down the street. Respect their individuality, their abilities, and their skills and let them know you appreciate them. Putting yourself in their shoes for a bit will allow you to be a greater person.

But don't overdo it. Be sincere. The recipient knows the difference, not simply from your words but from your manner toward people. It can be seen in your body language, your actions, and your ability to empathize. It can't be faked. We should all be sensitive to the fact that we are all sensitive.

Our need for respect does not only apply to people. Although George was already dead when our national anthem was written, he surely would have endorsed respectful behavior during its playing. Despite our grievances and complaints, this is one way we demonstrate our pride in and respect for our country.

Waiting in Line

Jill was inching up in a long line at the fast-food restaurant. Suddenly, a new order taker stepped up to the cash register, caught her eye, and said, "Ma'am, I'll take your order over here." Although it would have been easy to step to the front of a new line after being invited to do so, she replied, "The gentleman in front of me hasn't been helped yet either." With a grateful smile, the man in front of Jill shifted the small child he was holding in his arms, said thank you to her, and moved to the front of the new line.

Civility comes in small but thoughtful acts.

Address to the Continental Congress, June 16, 1775 (when informed he had been chosen to be general and commander in chief of the American forces): "THO' I AM TRULY SENSIBLE OF THE HIGH HONOR DONE ME IN THE APPOINTMENT, YET I FEEL GREAT DISTRESS, FROM A CONSCIOUSNESS THAT MY ABILITIES AND MILITARY EXPERIENCE MAY NOT BE EQUAL TO THE EXTENSIVE AND IMPORTANT TRUST."

WHEN IN COMPANY, PUT NOT YOUR HANDS TO ANY PART OF THE BODY NOT USUALLY DISCOVERED.

For shame! George has a unique way of saying it. (In his day, "discovered" in this context meant "displayed.") All scratching and kidding aside, he has a point. No one wants to see this. The rule applies to baseball players and rock stars as well.

SHOW NOTHING TO YOUR FRIEND THAT MAY AFFRIGHT HIM.

This rule is suspended during Halloween. Having served in two wars, GW saw some truly frightening events, so he no doubt knew the suffering fear can create. Just as friends don't let friends drive drunk, a friend doesn't make another friend's skin crawl, hair stand on end, or heart beat rapidly. Frightening someone is simply a cruel exercise of power—another form of disrespect. A thoughtful, civilized person thinks twice before bringing together the unsuspecting with spiders and reptiles. For those who want to indulge in the scary stuff, there are plenty of options—horror films and cable TV, just to name two.

Rule 4

IN THE PRESENCE OF OTHERS, SING NOT
TO YOURSELF WITH A HUMMING NOISE,
NOR DRUM WITH YOUR FINGERS OR FEET.

Unless you are Tony Bennett, Celine Dion, or Ringo Starr and have mounted the stage, avoid humming, drumming, and stomping. You annoy, distract, and insult those around you. George would be pleased to know that his rule has modern applications. Letting loud music blare from your open apartment window or car radio, for example, is singularly uncivilized, as are talking and fidgeting during movies.

There are modern exceptions to this rule. Stomping, clapping, and chanting while rooting for your favorite team is acceptable in our sports-oriented culture, as long as the words do not turn profane.

Rule 5

IF YOU COUGH, SNEEZE, SIGH, OR YAWN,
DO IT NOT LOUD BUT PRIVATELY; AND
SPEAK NOT IN YOUR YAWNING, BUT
PUT YOUR HANDKERCHIEF OR HAND
BEFORE YOUR FACE AND TURN ASIDE.

Although sometimes we are taken by surprise and cannot avoid transgressing, these are practices we learned in preschool. Sharing (another preschool lesson) does not apply to germs, so use a hanky or a tissue. Good manners and good hygiene go hand in hand. And if you do erupt in an explosive event, cover your mouth and excuse yourself. A yawn may be involuntary, but you can avoid speaking at the same time.

Rule 6

SLEEP NOT WHEN OTHERS SPEAK, SIT NOT WHEN OTHERS STAND, SPEAK NOT WHEN YOU SHOULD HOLD YOUR PEACE, WALK NOT ON WHEN OTHERS STOP.

GW covered a lot of ground with this rule—and you will too, if you adhere to these four admonitions, all of which have much to do with the respect George speaks of in Rule 1. Sleeping in the back of class, for example, shows little respect for the one up front and guarantees you a poor grade. Sitting while others stand will assure you hostile glances. Speaking when you should hold your peace may get you a piece of someone's mind. (But if you know when not to speak, seatmates on your bus, plane, or train are likely to be appreciative.) If you walk on when others stop, you'll soon be walking alone.

George Washington's second inaugural address, given in Philadelphia, was the shortest one ever; it was only 126 words.

Rule 7

PUT NOT OFF YOUR CLOTHES IN THE PRESENCE OF OTHERS, NOR GO OUT OF YOUR CHAMBER HALF DRESSED.

We wear far fewer layers of clothes than folks in the eighteenth century, and we think less of doing without a few of them—in certain circumstances. Clothes may not make the man (or woman), but taking them off indiscriminately may be your undoing. Even casual Fridays at the office have their limits.

AT PLAY AND AT FIRE IT'S GOOD MANNERS TO GIVE PLACE TO THE LAST COMER, AND AFFECT NOT TO SPEAK LOUDER THAN ORDINARY.

Arriving last is always a bit uncomfortable, so it's generous to include a latecomer in an activity that has already started, be it around the campfire or in a sport or card game. Welcome others as you would like to be welcomed. Last in a queue, however, is always last.

Speaking loudly, one of George's pet peeves, still offends all but the hard of hearing. Turn down the volume and use a civil and moderate tone—except in an emergency.

SPIT NOT INTO THE FIRE, NOR STOOP
LOW BEFORE IT, NEITHER PUT YOUR
HANDS INTO THE FLAMES TO WARM
THEM, NOR SET YOUR FEET UPON THE
FIRE, ESPECIALLY IF THERE BE MEAT
BEFORE IT.

We can translate this rule easily from the eighteenth
century; it instructs us to share the comforts. Don't block
the heat or the view and be aware of those around you.
Don't sit in front of someone in a near-empty movie theater. Watch out for your fellow celebrants on blankets at a
Fourth of July celebration. Consider those waiting to use
the pay phone or the rest room. Community is created by
sharing.

WHEN YOU SIT DOWN, KEEP YOUR FEET
FIRM AND EVEN, WITHOUT PUTTING
ONE ON THE OTHER OR CROSSING THEM.

The arrangement of your feet is no longer a matter of
civility provided they are not placed upon the furniture.
Cross your legs if it pleases you.

Rule 11

SHIFT NOT YOURSELF IN THE SIGHT OF OTHERS NOR GNAW YOUR NAILS.

Shift all you like, but back off on your fingernails. The disgusting and unsanitary habit of nail-biting, which GW (a credible source) indicates existed 250 years ago, ought to have been ended by now. Let's add cracking knuckles to the endangered-habit list as well.

Rule 12

SHAKE NOT YOUR HEAD, FEET, OR
LEGS, ROLL NOT THE EYES, LIFT NOT
ONE EYEBROW HIGHER THAN THE
OTHER, WRY NOT THE MOUTH, AND
BEDEW NO MAN'S FACE WITH YOUR
SPITTLE BY APPROACHING TOO NEAR
HIM WHEN YOU SPEAK.

Physical comments speak as loudly as verbal ones. Make every effort to hide feelings you might be tempted to express with parts of your body. Put a smile on your cynicism and be amused by the foibles of others. Don't use your face to register disagreement with someone's legitimate opinion. Do not pretend to tolerate differences of lifestyle while your body shows disapproval. And when you dispute, mind your saliva. Even the most vigorous of discussions should not result in a shower on your opponent's face. Stand back and swallow often.

Kill no vermin, as fleas, lice, ticks, etc., in the sight of others. If you see any filth or thick spittle, put your foot dexterously upon it; if it be upon the clothes of your companions, put if off privately; and if it be upon your own clothes, return thanks to him who puts it off.

We might think that, not being exterminators, we would have little use for this advice. But once we get past the odious vermin, the lesson is clearly valuable. When you help someone, do it quietly, without fanfare, and without expecting anything in return. Do acknowledge those who help you. It's nearly impossible to overuse "please" and "thank you," and the tone of your voice enhances your expression of appreciation. Please say the words meaningfully and often. Thank you.

The Flight Attendant

We were aloft. The flight attendant, who was beginning to serve beverages, asked the passengers pleasantly what they would like to drink. When she arrived at our row, the gentleman sitting next to me said, "Ginger ale, please." I asked, "May I have a Coke, please?" She smiled as she handed us our drinks. We each thanked her and she replied, "You're welcome."

She then turned to the woman on the other side of the aisle, who was reading a newspaper, and asked her what she would like to drink. Without looking up, the passenger responded, "Apple juice." The flight attendant looked at the woman, then slowly poured the juice into a cup and stood there holding it. After a few moments, the woman looked up. Nothing was said, but it was obvious the drink was not going to be served. Finally, the woman came to her civil senses. She thanked the flight attendant and was given the juice.

No matter how routine the situation, good manners are always good form.

TURN NOT YOUR BACK TO OTHERS, ESPECIALLY IN SPEAKING. JOG NOT THE TABLE OR DESK ON WHICH ANOTHER READS OR WRITES. LEAN NOT UPON ANYONE.

It's no coincidence that the expression "to turn one's back" has significance beyond the mere physical gesture. Establishing and maintaining eye contact is a sign of respect, politeness, and sincerity. Once you have begun a conversation, avoid being verbose. It's rude to monopolize another's time for the pleasure of hearing your own voice. On the flip side, be an attentive listener. Never interrupt. Be certain the speaker has finished before you begin. All good talk-show hosts follow this rule. It does require patience to learn to hear someone out, but it's what you would want for yourself. By listening patiently, you can figure out the solution to many a concern.

Jogging is for the running track. Walk carefully around the surfaces people are working on. GW's final prohibition was for physical leaning only. We all need someone we can lean on for help.

KEEP YOUR NAILS CLEAN AND SHORT, ALSO YOUR HANDS AND TEETH CLEAN, YET WITHOUT SHOWING ANY GREAT CONCERN FOR THEM.

We need no translation—or signs on the rest-room door—to remind us of the importance of cleanliness, which continues to be the mark of a civilized person. Concern in this area is also a matter of health. (Lest you misunderstand GW's final phrase in this rule, let me clarify: He means us to perform the necessary cleaning in private rather than in public.) Nowadays, you do not have to spend large amounts of time on personal hygiene, because of modern products and conveniences. Consistency of use is the key.

DO NOT PUFF UP THE CHEEKS, LOLL NOT OUT THE TONGUE WITH THE HANDS OR BEARD, THRUST NOT OUT THE LIPS OR BITE THEM, OR KEEP THE LIPS TOO OPEN OR TOO CLOSE.

This rule paints a graphic picture reminiscent of the gargoyles on medieval buildings. Perhaps GW knew people who unconsciously assumed one or more of these dreadful expressions. But more likely he refers to those who affect these grim visages (particularly the sticking out of one's tongue) for the purpose of ridiculing another—a tasteless practice that hurts the victim and diminishes the perpetrator.

Do not criticize the imperfections of others. Since we all have them, it is best to overlook them. Feel no envy. Be pleased with your own attributes and accomplishments.

Rule 17

BE NO FLATTERER; NEITHER PLAY WITH ANY THAT DELIGHT NOT TO BE PLAYED WITHAL.

An age of sincerity and candor has dawned once again. People want straight talk, honesty, and openness. Flattery has an element of exaggeration. A compliment, or words of praise, is one thing; flattery, which smacks of manipulation, is another. In time, most people see through flattery and begin to wonder what is behind the veil. Avoid the danger of being thought an opportunist. Speak plainly and without exaggeration, and avoid flattering or "kissing up" to those who find it a clear indication of insincerity.

Do not tease others. While some might be good-humored about it, many will be hurt. Most people, children and adults alike, do not appreciate being taunted in this way. There is no point in risking the possibility of hurting someone.

READ NO LETTERS, BOOKS, OR PAPERS
IN COMPANY, BUT WHEN THERE IS A
NECESSITY FOR THE DOING OF IT YOU
MUST LEAVE. COME NOT NEAR THE
BOOKS OR WRITINGS OF ANOTHER SO AS
TO READ THEM, UNLESS DESIRED, OR
GIVE YOUR OPINION OF THEM UNASKED.
ALSO LOOK NOT NIGH WHEN ANOTHER
IS WRITING A LETTER.

Respect and privacy—two sturdy threads of civility—
are woven together in this rule. Do not read in the presence of others unless the reason is compelling. Respect
the privacy of another's papers, messages, or work by not
reading or commenting on them unless you are asked. A
boss should not look over an employee's shoulder or at a
computer screen. Similarly, employees should avert their
eyes from the papers on the desk of a manager. Many
people forget that those closest to them—their spouses
and children—have a right to privacy as well. Don't be in
the doghouse. No one likes a snoop.

LET YOUR COUNTENANCE BE PLEASANT BUT IN SERIOUS MATTERS SOMEWHAT GRAVE.

In this rule, GW refers to facial expressions, which might be considered mere window dressing, but there's depth to his message. People who broadcast a smile throughout the day create happiness within and without; they are on a positive spiral that pulls others in. Their laughter is contagious—and only humans can catch it. Look for opportunities to spread cheer. Of course, there are times when gravity is appropriate. Know when a smile is not the best garb.

THE GESTURES OF THE BODY MUST BE SUITED TO THE DISCOURSE YOU ARE UPON.

Your body language should always be true to your purpose. If your nonverbal behavior does not match the verbal, you are being deceptive. Which will be believed?

REPROACH NONE FOR THE INFIRMITIES OF NATURE, NOR DELIGHT THEM THAT HAVE [THEM] IN MIND.

Often, embarrassment overcomes judgment and we avoid making eye contact with disabled or elderly people. By not looking at them, we fail to acknowledge their existence. They become non-people. We should all embrace the spirit of the Americans with Disabilities Act and treat those who are blind, deaf, in wheelchairs, or otherwise handicapped with the same respect and acknowledgment we give others. The passage of the act is a sign that our country is headed in the right direction in this area, but legislation is only a beginning. Friendly and helpful gestures are always appreciated. At the very least, it's up to us to look everyone we meet in the eye and send a message of respect from one human being to another.

SHEW NOT YOURSELF GLAD AT THE MISFORTUNE OF ANOTHER, THOUGH HE WERE YOUR ENEMY.

Although "enemy" may be a strong word to describe our everyday rivals, it's nonetheless hard not to gloat when the grocery store clerk rejects the credit card of the man who just elbowed his way in front of you.

True civility requires that we fine-tune our sense of empathy and try to understand and find compassion for the people who have hurt us as well as for the people we love. It is far more noble to attempt to understand and accept the limitations of the barbarian than to stoop to the barbarian's level.

Rule 23

WHEN YOU SEE A CRIME PUNISHED, YOU MAY BE INWARDLY PLEASED, BUT ALWAYS SHEW PITY TO THE SUFFERING OFFENDER.

As this rule tells us, George lived by a high standard of civility that, sadly, is uncommon in our days. We are more inclined to let it all hang out—to show our inner feelings and reactions quite plainly in our demeanor and behavior—even when we know they are not appropriate. Rise to a higher level of conduct. Make the difficult separation between what you feel and what you know you should show.

Rule 24

DO NOT LAUGH TOO LOUD OR TOO MUCH AT ANY PUBLIC SPECTACLE.

The days of hiding one's mirth behind a gloved hand, a hanky, or a fan are past. It is perfectly acceptable to laugh freely in private and in public—as long as it is not at the expense of others.

Rule 25

SUPERFLUOUS COMPLIMENTS AND ALL
AFFECTATION OF CEREMONY ARE TO BE
AVOIDED, YET WHERE DUE THEY ARE
NOT TO BE NEGLECTED.

It is startling to read a 250-year-old admonition against ingratiating and phony behavior. React with an appropriate portion of genuine admiration and do not pour on a sticky layer of goo just to get ahead and win favor. Be true to yourself while you spare the feelings of others. Acknowledge events and accomplishments with the honor they deserve. One further note: Do not stand on ceremony. Your feet will hurt after a while. Break through!

George Washington was not an aristocrat. He was a man who liked to puncture pomposity. After he left the presidency, Washington preferred the title "general" to "president."

IN PUTTING OFF YOUR HAT TO PERSONS
OF DISTINCTION, AS NOBLEMEN,
JUSTICES, CHURCHMEN, ETC., MAKE A
REVERENCE, BOWING MORE OR LESS
ACCORDING TO THE CUSTOM OF THE
BETTER BRED, AND QUALITY OF
PERSONS. AMONG YOUR EQUALS EXPECT
NOT ALWAYS THAT THEY SHOULD BEGIN
WITH YOU FIRST, BUT TO PULL OFF THE
HAT WHEN THERE IS NO NEED IS
AFFECTATION. IN THE MANNER OF
SALUTING AND RESALUTING, IN A WORD,
KEEP TO THE MOST USUAL CUSTOM.

We've put bowing, saluting (and resaluting), and iden-
tifying people as persons of distinction behind us, but
even today patronizing gestures should be avoided. Shake
hands with a moderate grip and extend a healthy greeting. As an expression of respect for our country, it is still
fitting to take off your hat when the colors are shown and
the national anthem is played. In fact, it is a good idea for

men to remove their hats indoors, as it serves no useful purpose and can be viewed as disrespectful. Rise when a judge enters the court to show respect for our judicial system, which may be imperfect but is far better than any other legal system or anarchy.

To the Citizens of Baltimore, April 17, 1789: "IT APPEARS TO ME THAT LITTLE MORE THAN COMMON SENSE AND COMMON HONESTY, IN THE TRANSACTIONS OF THE COMMUNITY AT LARGE, WOULD BE NECESSARY TO MAKE US A GREAT AND HAPPY NATION."

Rule 27

'TIS ILL MANNERS TO BID ONE MORE
EMINENT THAN YOURSELF BE
COVERED, AS WELL AS NOT TO DO IT
TO WHOM IT IS DUE. LIKEWISE, HE
THAT MAKES TOO MUCH HASTE TO
PUT ON HIS HAT DOES NOT WELL.
YET HE OUGHT TO PUT IT ON AT THE
FIRST, OR AT MOST THE SECOND TIME
OF BEING ASKED. NOW WHAT IS
HEREIN SPOKEN, OF QUALIFICATION
IN BEHAVIOR IN SALUTING, OUGHT
ALSO TO BE OBSERVED IN TAKING OF
PLACE AND SITTING DOWN, FOR
CEREMONIES WITHOUT BOUNDS
ARE TROUBLESOME.

How alien this all seems to us! How mannered and irrelevant. True, we live in a (more or less) classless society, at least in terms of the speed of putting on your hat. But if you discard the frilly language and transform the "one more eminent than yourself" into your professor, boss, or manager, this rule may suddenly take on a more modern look. A wise person observes and respects the "ceremonies" that are meaningful to a superior—and to all others.

IF ANYONE COME TO SPEAK TO YOU WHILE YOU ARE SITTING, STAND UP, THOUGH HE BE YOUR INFERIOR, AND WHEN YOU PRESENT SEATS, LET IT BE TO EVERYONE ACCORDING TO HIS DEGREE.

Class consciousness, which permeated the eighteenth century, manifested itself in many ways, including sitting and standing "according to degree." We no longer sit and stand on ceremony, but we ought to join a person with whom we are conversing at that person's level. It's not only polite, it avoids neck strain! As a gesture of respect and deference, younger people ought to offer seats to older people on public transportation and in private accommodations.

WHEN YOU MEET WITH ONE OF GREATER QUALITY THAN YOURSELF, STOP AND RETIRE, ESPECIALLY IF IT BE AT A DOOR OR ANY STRAIGHT PLACE, TO GIVE WAY FOR HIM TO PASS.

Although the basis of this rule—people of greater and lesser quality—is antiquated, we can still make good use of the principle by yielding to people in wheelchairs or on crutches, the elderly, and people with small children. Follow the lead of the airlines.

Rule 30

IN WALKING, THE HIGHEST PLACE IN
MOST COUNTRIES SEEMS TO BE ON THE
RIGHT HAND, THEREFORE, PLACE
YOURSELF ON THE LEFT OF HIM WHOM
YOU DESIRE TO HONOR. BUT IF THREE
WALK TOGETHER, THE MIDDLE PLACE IS
THE MOST HONORABLE. THE WALL IS
USUALLY GIVEN TO THE MORE WORTHY
IF TWO WALK TOGETHER.

This musty practice was probably very important to those who hung out with royalty. Unless you do, you can ignore it and walk alongside your companion without heed as to right and left. The key is to be attentive to your fellow walker.

IF ANYONE FAR SURPASSES OTHERS EITHER IN AGE, ESTATE, OR MERIT, YET WOULD GIVE PLACE TO A MEANER ONE THAN HIMSELF, THE ONE OUGHT NOT TO ACCEPT IT. SO HE ON THE OTHER PART SHOULD NOT USE MUCH EARNESTNESS NOR OFFER IT ABOVE ONCE OR TWICE.

According to GW's rule, someone of a meaner (lower) class was to refuse the place offered by someone of greater age, wealth, or station. Although we've abandoned the rank idea of rank, a generous gesture by someone of means to someone who is less fortunate should be lauded. It is an act of great civility to treat another with empathy and kindness.

Learning from the Best

When I was a rookie lawyer, I had the good fortune of being invited to the office of Mr. Murdoch, a well-established and highly respected real estate attorney and a grand master in the local bar association. The event was an estate closing, in which a house or other piece of real estate was to change hands.

Being new to the profession and aware of this man's seniority in the field, I felt nervous and intimidated as I entered his staid old law office and thanked him for agreeing to allow me to observe. He immediately took me into the conference room and introduced me to the buyers and sellers. Then, looking at me over his half glasses, he asked if I wanted a cup of coffee. I said I would if it was not too much trouble.

With that, he walked to a side room and returned with a cup, which he graciously handed to me. He did not ask a secretary, law clerk, or legal assistant to serve me the coffee; he poured it and served it himself. I felt myself relax.

Even before the legal proceedings began, I learned something from this important and gracious man: Treat juniors with grace and civility, and be sure that a newcomer is made comfortable in an awkward situation.

TO ONE THAT IS YOUR EQUAL OR NOT MUCH INFERIOR, YOU ARE TO GIVE THE CHIEF PLACE IN YOUR LODGING, AND HE TO WHOM 'TIS OFFERED OUGHT AT THE FIRST TO REFUSE IT BUT AT THE SECOND TO ACCEPT, THOUGH NOT WITHOUT ACKNOWLEDGING HIS OWN UNWORTHINESS.

Is this why there are so many signs that say GEORGE WASHINGTON SLEPT HERE? A generous spirit of hospitality is one of the hallmarks of a civil society. Offer the best to your guest—not once but twice. The civil guest should graciously accept, certainly on the second offer—as GW (a modest man who was conscious of his own "unworthiness") must have done often.

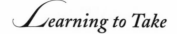Learning to Take

Many people spend a great deal of time living in accordance with the adage that it is better to give than to receive. They may end up never being *able* to receive. It is important to both give and receive graciously. When you receive something graciously, the person who has given feels good. When you give, you derive pleasure from the recipient's joy. The avenue of giving and receiving should not be a one-way street.

THEY THAT ARE IN DIGNITY OR IN
OFFICE HAVE IN ALL PLACES
PRECEDENCY, BUT WHILST THEY ARE
YOUNG THEY OUGHT TO RESPECT THOSE
THAT ARE THEIR EQUALS IN BIRTH OR
OTHER QUALITIES, THOUGH THEY HAVE
NO PUBLIC CHARGE.

YIELD is a good sign for many intersections on the road of life. Develop the habit of holding the door open, of stopping to let others pass, of allowing others to speak first if you both start together, and of excusing yourself if you bump into someone. And those who yield to you ought to be suitably and audibly thanked.

The Highway Commuter

Joan commuted by car from her home in the suburbs to the city. The highway was always crowded and the heavy traffic crept along bumper-to-bumper. Even on days she started out early, she arrived barely on time.

On this particular morning in the middle of an exhausting week, Joan left home when it was not quite light and the early commuters were traveling with their lights on. She had to be aggressive as she entered from the on ramp, even though her signal was on.

Once on the highway, she was a courteous, civil driver. She allowed others on the road by yielding. She let people who needed to change lanes do so ahead of her. She did not tailgate and she always signaled when she was about to change lanes. All this cost her nothing, and some drivers returned the favors. Some waved in her direction in appreciation as they passed. Joan mused on their need to thank her. She felt she was doing the decent thing, acting responsibly and being considerate.

We are all on the highway together.

Rule 34

IT IS GOOD MANNERS TO PREFER
THEM TO WHOM WE SPEAK BEFORE
OURSELVES, ESPECIALLY IF THEY BE
ABOVE US, WITH WHOM IN NO SORT
WE OUGHT TO BEGIN.

Above or below—this has no bearing today. But if we are to the manor born—and have good manners, we graciously let the other person speak first and, when others are speaking, permit them their point of view. It isn't always necessary to contradict or force a confrontation if you disagree.

From a Letter to John Sullivan, May 11, 1781: "IT IS MUCH EASIER TO AVOID DISAGREEMENTS THAN TO REMOVE DISCONTENTS."

LET YOUR DISCOURSE WITH MEN OF BUSINESS BE SHORT AND COMPREHENSIVE.

This rule is even more timely now than when George wrote it, because, of course, we have less time. More time on the planet, for most of us, but less unscheduled time in each day. Point: Be short and sweet in business. It is inconsiderate to waste the time of others. Keep your voice-mail messages short; keep your e-mails short; keep your presentations short. Short—and substantive. When you make a presentation, know your material so well you can boil it down to its essence.

And don't frivolously extend discussions initiated by others. Disagree or question only when the matter is of extreme importance—not just because you haven't been heard at a particular meeting and you want the boss to know you're there.

Letter to Marquis de Lafayette, August 15, 1786: "... HOW-EVER UNIMPORTANT AMERICA MAY BE CONSIDERED AT PRESENT, AND HOWEVER BRITAIN MAY AFFECT TO DESPISE HER TRADE, THERE WILL ASSUREDLY COME A DAY, WHEN THIS COUNTRY WILL HAVE SOME WEIGHT IN THE SCALE OF EMPIRES."

ARTIFICERS AND PERSONS OF LOW DEGREE OUGHT NOT TO USE MANY CEREMONIES TO LORDS OR OTHERS OF HIGH DEGREE, BUT RESPECT AND HIGHLY HONOR THEM, AND THOSE OF HIGH DEGREE OUGHT TO TREAT THEM WITH AFFABILITY AND COURTESY, WITHOUT ARROGANCY.

When we examine this rule through a modern monocle that screens out references to artificers (tricksters) and persons of low and high degree, we see advice we can relate to our daily lives. Regardless of the station of the people we come in contact with, look for the common denominator and respond accordingly. Behave naturally, respecting all, including the people you report to and those who report to you. Ingratiating and fawning behavior sounds a sour note when we are conducting business and engaging in social activities, and an attitude of arrogance curdles the air between us. No matter how much you achieve, do not assume a cloak of superiority; remain human and humble.

In speaking to men do not lean nor look them full in the face, nor approach too near them. At least keep a full pace from them.

Then and now we all need our space. It can be annoying, intimidating, or even threatening to have someone edge up too close to you. It is certainly uncivil. I doubt that many of us intentionally invade the space of others. However, a gentle reminder: Different people have different levels of comfort with physical familiarity. Try to tune in and err on the side of respectful distance.

A SHORT TALE OF CIVILITY

At the Bank

I was in line at the bank. When my turn came, I waved hello to Ms. Williams, a friendly teller I have known for years who was at the window next to me.

The woman next in line went to Ms. Williams's window and handed her a check to be cashed. Ms. Williams politely explained that it was bank policy not to cash large checks for people who did not have accounts there. Proper identification and a fingerprint were necessary. Upon hearing this, the woman exploded in a series of profanities, berating both the teller and the bank.

Ms. Williams continued to explain the policy and was treated to another outburst of expletives. Appalled by her conduct, I turned to the woman and told her she was being rude and inappropriate. She gave me a surprised look and told me to mind my own business. When I apologized to Ms. Williams on the woman's behalf, the woman actually told her not to accept the apology. Just then the bank manager came over and asked the woman to leave immediately. Later, I was told that the manager barred her from ever returning.

When I reflected on this incident, it occurred to me that more people should have stepped forward to back me up. The word must go out that uncivilized behavior will not be tolerated. If more of us stand up for what is right, there will be tremendous social pressure to behave properly. Call it the "civility defense squad."

Rule 38

IN VISITING THE SICK, DO NOT PRESENTLY PLAY THE PHYSICIAN IF YOU BE NOT KNOWING THEREIN.

Don't misrepresent yourself when offering advice. If you must provide guidance in an area in which you are not well versed, couch your advice in terms that makes clear you are a novice: "I'm not an expert, but . . . "

In a broader sense, act with honesty and candor. Don't fake it. Here's a tip: Three little words that are among the most difficult to say are also the most freeing. Are you ready? Here they are: "I don't know." (To be followed by, when appropriate, "but I'll find someone who does know and will learn with you.")

And by the way, don't offer advice in the first place unless you're asked.

Rule 39

IN WRITING OR SPEAKING, GIVE TO EVERY PERSON HIS DUE TITLE ACCORDING TO HIS DEGREE AND THE CUSTOM OF THE PLACE.

In George's time, a "due title" was likely to be inherited—and likely to play an important role in one's social standing. And those titles were frequently cited because formalities of writing and speech were carefully observed. Some of that formality has disappeared from our social surroundings and we tend to be more casual in our modes of address, both written and spoken. Nevertheless, despite the fact that we are likely to bear titles that have been earned by our academic efforts or in our careers, it is still proper to give the appropriate acknowledgment.

Taking this idea one step further, and into the work world, strive to give others positive feedback so they know when they have performed well. When they haven't, constructive criticism can go a long way toward giving them a push in the right direction. You can make a responsive and mature environment the "custom" of your "place."

Rule 40

STRIVE NOT WITH YOUR SUPERIORS IN ARGUMENT, BUT ALWAYS SUBMIT YOUR JUDGMENT TO OTHERS IN MODESTY.

Be careful, be circumspect, be civil. If you disagree, don't argue defensively. Listen carefully to what is being said, and respond as vigorously as you wish, but with diplomatic restraint and consideration. Using soft language such as "It seems to me" or "It might be that" shows that you recognize other views are feasible. And consider this: Focus your attention always on the points being discussed and not on the person doing the discussing. When you find yourself judging the *person*, that's the time to stop talking, take a breath, and regroup.

UNDERTAKE NOT TO TEACH YOUR EQUAL IN THE ART HE HIMSELF PROFESSES; IT SAVORS OF ARROGANCY.

Take a time-honored tip from GW: Resist the urge to give advice. It smacks of arrogance and reeks of disrespect. Listen carefully when you think your advice is being sought; you may be mistaken. The words "Let me ask your advice" may be only a means of releasing a cloudburst of complaints. Advice is often offered but seldom welcome.

Arrogance serves no purpose in this or any other situation. True self-confidence engenders respect for self and others, whereas arrogance sets up a power play. Find the balance between confidence and arrogance and do not tip the teeter-totter: Feel good about yourself but keep your ego in check.

Letter to Benjamin Franklin, October 18, 1782: "I AM MUCH OBLIGED BY THE POLITICAL INFORMATION WHICH YOU HAVE TAKEN THE TROUBLE TO CONVEY TO ME, BUT FEEL MYSELF MUCH EMBARRASSED IN MY WISH TO MAKE YOU A RETURN IN KIND."

LET YOUR CEREMONIES IN COURTESY
BE PROPER TO THE DIGNITY OF HIS
PLACE WITH WHOM YOU CONVERSE,
FOR IT IS ABSURD TO ACT THE SAME
WITH A CLOWN AND A PRINCE.

George wrote these rules before he commanded the revolutionary troops against the British. In his colonial society, firm distinctions were made between a "clown" (by which he meant a country bumpkin) and a prince (which meant a lot more than a prince of a fellow). Society has changed in ways GW would never have imagined. In our melting pot, we strive to erase distinctions based on economics, race, gender, and origin, rather than preserve them and base our relationships on them.

Despite the changes in society, however, we would do well to pick and choose among GW's words and act on them: Be courteous and proper, as he advises, but respect the dignity of *all* those with whom you converse. Treat all equally well. The strength in our country comes from diversity and our belief in a civility based on consideration, sensitivity, kindness, and tolerance, which in essence is not that far from what George believed. Don't be a country bumpkin (awkward and unsophisticated). Pay homage to the greatness of our country's past by valuing and respecting every citizen. In other words, to be civil is to be cool.

Judging People

A woman in a faded gingham dress and her husband, dressed in a homespun threadbare suit, stepped off the train in Boston and walked timidly without an appointment into the Harvard University president's outer office. The secretary could tell in a moment that such backwoods country hicks had no business at Harvard and probably didn't even deserve to be in Cambridge. She frowned.

"We want to see the president," the man said softly.

"He'll be busy all day," the secretary snapped.

"We'll wait," the woman replied.

For hours, the secretary ignored them, hoping the couple would become discouraged and go away. When they didn't the secretary grew frustrated and finally decided to disturb the president, even though it was a chore she always regretted.

"Maybe if they just see you for a few minutes, they'll leave," she told him. He sighed in exasperation and nodded. Someone of his importance obviously didn't have the time to spend with them, but he detested gingham dresses and homespun suits cluttering up his outer office. Stern-faced with dignity, the president strutted toward the couple.

The woman told him, "We had a son who attended Harvard for one year. He loved Harvard. He was happy here. But about a year ago he was accidentally killed. My husband and I would like to erect a memorial to him, somewhere on campus."

The president wasn't touched; he was shocked.

"Madam," he said gruffly, "we can't put up a statue for every person who attended Harvard and died. If we did, this place would look like a cemetery."

"Oh, no," the woman explained quickly. "We don't want to erect a statue. We thought we would like to give a building to Harvard."

The president rolled his eyes. He glanced at the gingham dress and homespun suit and then exclaimed, "A building! Do you have any earthly idea how much a building costs? We have over seven and a half million dollars in the physical plant at Harvard."

For a moment the woman was silent. The president was pleased. He could get rid of them now. Then she turned to her husband and said quietly, "Is that all it costs to build a university? Why don't we just start our own?"

Her husband nodded. The president's face wilted in

confusion and bewilderment. And Mr. and Mrs. Leland Stanford walked out and went to Palo Alto, California, where they established the university that bears their name as a memorial to a son that Harvard no longer cared about.

You can easily judge the character of others by how they treat those who they think can do nothing for them or to them.

<hr>

Although he founded a great university, George Washington never went to college. He had the least schooling of any of the Founding Fathers, most of whom had gone to university in Great Britain. Although he did not have the benefit of higher education, he loved to read and learn.

<hr>

DO NOT EXPRESS JOY BEFORE ONE SICK IN PAIN, FOR THE CONTRARY PASSION WILL AGGRAVATE HIS MISERY.

The key to so many interpersonal situations, including this one, is empathy. Turn on your wide bandwidth and tune all your senses to the ill person's signals. How will your broadcast be received? Will your efforts to uplift a flagging spirit be heard? How much joviality is appropriate? And then moderate your mood and your message of sympathy to proper volume and stay only as long as you are welcome.

Be sure to check on friends and relatives who have been ill and be willing to supply what is needed if they are unable to provide for themselves. The hospital room is often a cheerless, impersonal place. Visitors can break up the endless day and bring cheer, but do not stay more than twenty minutes. Several short visits will bring more healing than one interminable one.

At Peace

Bill's friend Rick had terminal cancer, and Rick's wife, Sally, was trying to do all she could for him in his final months.

One of Rick's pleasures in life was boating. He had often motored in his small boat on a beautiful lake near his home, but when he became ill he had sold the boat. Sally called Bill's wife, Ruth, and a day on the lake on Bill's boat was arranged.

The couples got together on a perfect spring day. Rick, pale and thin, enjoyed himself as they floated leisurely on the water and soaked up the sun and the scenery. At the end of the day, Rick and Sally thanked Bill and Ruth.

A week later, Bill visited Rick at his home. They talked about the lake, fishing, and boats—and of the lovely day they had spent together. Ten days later, Bill died. A few days after the funeral, Sally called Bill to thank him again for the day on the lake and for not discussing Rick's illness during his visit. Bill replied that Rick did not bring it up so neither did he.

Generosity and empathy—two attributes of civility Bill showed toward his dying friend—are always appreciated.

WHEN A MAN DOES ALL HE CAN, THOUGH IT SUCCEEDS NOT WELL, BLAME HIM NOT THAT DID IT.

Commendation—not criticism—is called for when one makes a good effort. Blame is like rubbing salt in the wound of a person who has labored unsuccessfully. Failure is its own punishment. A friend offers a gentle word of empathy and a boost to the deflated spirit.

A good-faith attempt—and persistence in the face of failure—is always the first step on the road to success. After winning one term in the U.S. House of Representatives, Abraham Lincoln lost his bid for reelection. Six years later, he lost yet another election when he ran for the Senate. He persisted. Five years later, in 1860, he was elected as the sixteenth president.

Although this rule is pertinent to many occasions, it is particularly applicable to sporting events. When your team loses, never point a finger at one player, who no doubt has already taken on a large share of the blame. Children are particularly prone to believe they are responsible for a team's failures. It's important to cite their efforts and that of their teammates to right the listing ship.

BEING TO ADVISE OR REPREHEND
ANYONE, CONSIDER WHETHER IT
OUGHT TO BE IN PUBLIC OR IN PRIVATE,
PRESENTLY OR AT SOME OTHER TIME,
IN WHAT TERMS TO DO IT, AND IN
REPROVING SHOW NO SIGN OF CHOLER
[ANGER], BUT DO IT WITH ALL
SWEETNESS AND MILDNESS.

People who are being criticized constructively listen better when the language is soft, the tone is quiet, and the setting is private. There is nothing more humiliating than a loud public reprimand—and, for that matter, nothing more damaging to the person doing the reprimanding. No matter how justified, public criticism always hurts the person criticizing more than the wrongdoer; it's human nature to feel sympathy for the one being berated.

I think this advice is especially useful for parents. Some of us who would never think to publicly reprimand an adult do so without a thought when a child misbehaves. A child can be just as humiliated as an adult. Take the time and the energy to remove the child from the situation and talk quietly about the inappropriate behavior. You will be giving your child respect as well as discipline, and you will be setting an example of civilized behavior.

Constructive Criticism

I felt my knees knocking that day in court. It was my first jury trial and I was very nervous. Judge John McAuliffe, known to be brilliant and thorough, was sitting. It was over in the afternoon and the jury returned a verdict in our favor.

Emboldened by my success, I approached the judge and told him the trial was my very first. He immediately responded from the bench that it didn't show. I thanked him for that gracious remark.

This same judge took me aside at a bar association meeting a few days later and told me I might be a little less long-winded when I spoke to a jury. I thanked him again.

TAKE ALL ADMONITIONS THANKFULLY IN WHAT TIME OR PLACE SOEVER GIVEN, BUT AFTERWARDS, NOT BEING CULPABLE, TAKE A TIME AND PLACE CONVENIENT TO LET HIM KNOW IT THAT GAVE THEM.

Be sure to thank a well-intentioned person for warning you of some condition that threatens you. If that condition turns out not to exist or has ceased to exist, you should let your source know. In that way, others will not be misled. Even if you say nothing, the warning is still very nice. In any event, an expression of gratitude to someone who looks out for you is the mark of a civil person.

It is a selfless other-directed act to look out for others. By not doing so, you are being self-centered, which will cause you to mistreat others even if unintended. Dwelling on yourself will deny you the opportunity to enjoy others and they you.

MOCK NOT NOR JEST AT ANYTHING OF IMPORTANCE, BREAK NO JESTS THAT ARE SHARP AND BITING, AND IF YOU DELIVER ANYTHING WITTY AND PLEASANT, ABSTAIN FROM LAUGHING THEREAT YOURSELF.

Although we all like to leave them laughing, jokes and jests can be nasty tools in the wrong hands and at the wrong time. When the mood is solemn, an ill-timed quip can bring the curtain down—on your head! Ridicule, pranks, and wisecracks diminish the joker and evoke a chorus of boos. Satire and parody are best left to polished performers in the theater.

Although it is often said, Laugh and the world laughs with you, fine comics only smile inwardly at their own witticisms and enjoy the pleasure that others get from their jokes and stories. At the very least, if you do laugh be sure you are not the only person doing so. If you must laugh, join in after the others have started.

And, finally, learn to laugh at yourself. Self-deprecating humor is a blessing that keeps your ego in check, the world in perspective, and the curtain going up.

Rule 48

WHEREIN YOU REPROVE ANOTHER BE UNBLAMABLE YOURSELF, FOR EXAMPLE IS MORE PREVALENT THAN PRECEPTS.

You've no doubt heard these two ideas before: "Let him that is without sin cast the first stone" and "Actions speak louder than words." GW has woven them together for a doubly potent bit of advice to remind us to look to our own behavior before that of others.

Here's another way of expressing the first concept: Don't attempt to remove a speck from your brother's eye when there is a log in your own. Most of us see the short-comings of others as much bigger than our own—if we see ours at all. Turn the magnifying glass around and scrutinize your own behavior before decrying that of others.

The second thought encourages us to lead by example. Civil people undertake to act in a civil manner and to refrain from casting blame. They are more inclined to excuse the uncivil behavior of others by attributing it to some temporary factor (such as confusion, ill health, or fatigue) rather than malevolence or selfishness.

This double-duty rule is worth a great deal of consideration. Incorporate it into your everyday activities and note the results.

USE NO REPROACHFUL LANGUAGE AGAINST ANYONE, NEITHER CURSE NOR REVILE.

You are alone in the house, attending to chores and making repairs. Suddenly you drop the hammer squarely on your small toe. Your yelp of pain is followed by a string of swearwords and curses. In that circumstance, it's difficult for even the most civil of us to contain an explosion of profanity. But otherwise, we would be much better off curbing our tongues. Profanity demeans *us*, not those against whom we use it. And it usually backfires. Those on the receiving end react angrily and defensively.

In any situation, but especially in a professional or business setting, restrain your raw and indelicate tongue. Lower the volume control. Speak with purpose and force if necessary but omit the vulgarities.

Losing the Argument

It is said that George Washington was sitting at the dinner table one evening with some of his relatives, enjoying a good conversation. Suddenly one of the men started to argue a point with one of the others. Every other word he used was profane. George, always mindful of civility, turned to him and remarked that he must have a very weak argument indeed if he needed to rely on profanity instead of words of substance to sway his opponent.

BE NOT HASTY TO BELIEVE FLYING REPORTS TO THE DISPARAGEMENT OF ANY.

Although tabloids like the *Star* and the *National Enquirer* didn't exist in George's day, it appears rumors and disparaging reports proliferated as frequently as they do today. Now, as then, "flying reports" ought to fall on deaf ears and should certainly not be given an additional lift. Ignore gossip and rumors. Squelch them if you can by going to the source to get accurate information. Never speak ill of others or launch a false or unsubstantiated story.

Those who desire to hear bad news about others are a sorry lot. I hope you don't count such people among your acquaintances. Feeling sorry for someone who has had a hard time or is in a bad way is an empathetic and civil emotion. Follow it up by seeing what you can do to help.

WEAR NOT YOUR CLOTHES FOUL, RIPT,
OR DUSTY, BUT SEE THEY BE BRUSHED
ONCE EVERY DAY AT LEAST AND TAKE
HEED THAT YOU APPROACH NOT TO
ANY UNCLEANNESS.

Preteens and teens are exempt from this rule. Ripped and well-worn clothes are badges of belonging for this age group. For the rest of us, clean well-cared-for clothes are required. George and his contemporaries had it a lot harder than we do. In their time, clothes were much fussier than today and washing machines were yet to be invented. So enjoy the luxury of our modern methods and the wonderful smell and feel of well-washed garb.

IN YOUR APPAREL BE MODEST
AND ENDEAVOR TO ACCOMMODATE
NATURE, RATHER THAN TO PROCURE
ADMIRATION. KEEP TO THE FASHION OF
YOUR EQUALS, SUCH AS ARE CIVIL AND
ORDERLY WITH RESPECT TO TIMES
AND PLACES.

Those under twenty-five are exempt from this rule as well. Like many people today, George preferred the natural look over the glamorous one. He probably also believed that clothes are not as important as the person who dons them. There are some who subscribe to the anything-goes and the more-outrageous-the-better school of dressing. Although in the minority, they are often in the public eye, taking advantage of this era of more personal freedom. If you remember that what you wear sends a message and you choose clothes that are appropriate for the occasion, you won't ever be out of style.

Rule 53

RUN NOT IN THE STREETS, NEITHER GO
TOO SLOWLY NOR WITH MOUTH OPEN.
GO NOT SHAKING YOUR ARMS, KICK
NOT THE EARTH WITH YOUR FEET,
GO NOT UPON THE TOES NOR IN A
DANCING FASHION.

GW was not thinking of joggers when he composed this rule. Physical activity in the streets in his time was much more regulated. Today, we delight in seeing children and adults on bicycles, neighbors out jogging or walking, parents pushing carriages, pet owners walking dogs, and letter carriers delivering mail—just to mention a few of those who make our neighborhoods lively and festive. Bike races, foot races, and farmers' markets help restore our lost sense of community.

PLAY NOT THE PEACOCK, LOOKING EVERYWHERE ABOUT TO SEE IF YOU BE WELL-DECKED, IF YOUR SHOES FIT WELL, IF YOUR STOCKINGS SIT NEATLY AND CLOTHES HANDSOMELY.

Peacocks belong in zoos or on the lawns of baronial mansions. Vanity is an unbecoming trait that smacks of self-absorption. Pay heed to the condition of your clothes and check that all buttons are buttoned and all zippers zipped, but beyond the basics of presentability lie showiness and swagger. Measure your moments before the mirror.

From a Letter to Bushrod Washington, January 15, 1783:
"DO NOT CONCEIVE THAT FINE CLOTHES MAKE FINE MEN, ANY MORE THAN FINE FEATHERS MAKE FINE BIRDS. A PLAIN, GENTEEL DRESS IS MORE ADMIRED."

Rule 55

EAT NOT IN THE STREETS NOR IN THE HOUSE, OUT OF SEASON.

Eating meals at regular intervals—whether at home or not—is still a sound practice. (In George's time, "out of season" did not refer to seasons of the year. He meant consuming food at regular intervals.)

Rule 56

ASSOCIATE YOURSELF WITH MEN OF GOOD QUALITY IF YOU ESTEEM YOUR OWN REPUTATION; FOR 'TIS BETTER TO BE ALONE THAN IN BAD COMPANY.

A couple of truisms apply here: (1) You are judged by the company you keep; and (2) If you lie down with dogs, you rise up with fleas. I believe that when Washington referred to "men of good quality" he could just as accurately have written "civilized men." Associate yourself with people who are truly civil: honest, caring, loyal, trustworthy, and empathetic. Be a person who can be counted on, and count on people like yourself.

Rule 57

IN WALKING UP AND DOWN IN A HOUSE, WITH ONLY ONE IN COMPANY, IF HE BE GREATER THAN YOURSELF, AT THE FIRST GIVE HIM THE RIGHT HAND AND STOP NOT TILL HE DOES AND BE NOT THE FIRST THAT TURNS, AND WHEN YOU DO LET IT BE WITH YOUR FACE TOWARD HIM. IF HE BE A MAN OF GREAT QUALITY, WALK NOT WITH HIM CHEEK BY JOWL BUT SOMEWHAT BEHIND, BUT YET IN SUCH A MANNER THAT HE MAY EASILY SPEAK TO YOU.

Although we no longer need to be concerned about our physical position in relation to someone we are walking with, a look at the detail of this rule gives us some idea of how important GW thought it was. A civilized person in Washington's time thought a great deal about even the smallest aspects of behavior. Perhaps we ought to think just a bit more than we do today about ours.

LET YOUR CONVERSATION BE WITHOUT MALICE OR ENVY AS A SIGN OF A COMMENDABLE NATURE.

Spare others from words tinged by envy and malice, even when you find yourself in the company of those who flaunt their riches and accomplishments and those who provoke nastiness. Display a commendable nature and earn the respect of others by avoiding words of jealousy. Live your own life—without malice or ill will, or envy toward others—and you will live longer and be happier.

On the flip side of this coin, be willing to praise others for their accomplishments but feel inwardly secure, whether or not you are acknowledged for your accomplishments and good deeds. Doing good is its own reward.

NEVER EXPRESS ANYTHING UNBECOMING NOR ACT AGAINST THE MORAL RULES BEFORE YOUR INFERIORS.

The civil boss should not be bossy, arrogant, or condescending. In the world of power politics, managers who treat those who work for them with respect, civility, and decency are in turn respected and admired. When he was chosen to be general and commander in chief—the boss—of the American forces, GW wrote of the "extensive and important Trust" he felt had been bestowed upon him. How many bosses feel that way today?

A further note of advice: Hold fast to your moral standards in the workplace and watch them suffuse those who work for you and with you. Your moral tone will have wide-reaching effects.

In the absence of his father (who died when he was eleven) and in contention with his mother, George Washington was guided in his personal conduct by these rules. All his life he held fast to his moral standards.

Rule 60

BE NOT IMMODEST IN URGING YOUR FRIENDS TO DISCOVER A SECRET.

Although the word "immodest" had little to do with sexual mores in GW's time, all of us today (and especially those who work at and read the tabloids) would be wise to take a cue from this rule. A secret revealed is no longer a secret. Prying and urging others to pry into people's lives is thoughtless and uncivilized.

Rule 61

UTTER NOT BASE AND FRIVOLOUS
THINGS AMONG GRAVE AND LEARNED
MEN, NOR VERY DIFFICULT QUESTIONS
OR SUBJECTS AMONG THE IGNORANT,
OR THINGS HARD TO BE BELIEVED.
STUFF NOT YOUR DISCOURSE WITH
SENTENCES AMONG YOUR BETTERS
NOR EQUALS.

Coarse and base language, which reveals the crude lower side of humanity, has no place in a truly civil society. Curb your tongue and, when necessary, admonish others to curb theirs. Stand against public displays of foul language, even among those who are not "grave and learned." In particular, shield young and delicate ears from bolts of profanity and thunderstorms of obscenity. The echo from a child's mouth is truly shocking.

Avoid pretense and do not speak above people's heads. Remain credible. Plain speaking is still a virtue.

At the Hockey Game

One night our whole family was enjoying a live hockey game. We were part of a large excited crowd that greeted the home team with roars of approval.

The game began with some brisk action. Not long into the first period, a loud voice from several rows behind yelled a stream of obscenities at our goalie. We all quieted down and listened in disbelief. The barrage of foul language continued.

A man one row behind us called out to the man who was uttering the profanities, "Hey, we didn't come to the game to listen to your foul mouth!" The man retorted, "I paid for a ticket just like everyone else. I can say whatever I want."

Though my wife was cringing, I stood up and turned around. "You are wrong," I said, pointing to the offender. "We are all here to enjoy the game, and we don't want to listen to your filthy language."

He glowered at me, but his demeanor changed abruptly when virtually everyone in our section turned toward him and voiced their agreement. It was a great feeling. Even in his drunken state this man was intimidated into acting properly for the rest of the game.

When it is safe to do so, we must back each other up when it comes to violations of civil behavior.

SPEAK NOT OF DOLEFUL THINGS IN A
TIME OF MIRTH OR AT THE TABLE;
SPEAK NOT OF MELANCHOLY THINGS
AS DEATH AND WOUNDS, AND IF
OTHERS MENTION THEM, CHANGE IF
YOU CAN THE DISCOURSE. TELL NOT
YOUR DREAMS BUT TO YOUR
INTIMATE FRIEND.

Even in George's time, no one liked a wet blanket. There is no substitute for good judgment in choosing the subject of a conversation. A splash of sadness and woe at a time of happiness can drown a happy crowd. Measure your words and tone before unleashing them. Note the emphasis on being upbeat at the table and of redirecting those who insist on pulling a buoyant group down.

And speaking of "telling" moments, George advises you to hold your hopes and dreams close to your heart. Only those closest to you should be privy to them.

A MAN OUGHT NOT TO VALUE HIMSELF OF HIS ACHIEVEMENTS OR RARE QUALITIES OF WIT, MUCH LESS OF HIS RICHES, VIRTUE, OR KINDRED.

Modesty, one of the great virtues of the past, has fallen out of favor. GW, the ultimate model of modesty, would certainly have agreed with Confucius that the "superior man is modest in his speech but exceeds in actions." Wrap your good deeds and achievements in a cloak of understated cloth, but persist in amassing a great number of them. Value your attempts to be a good human being, to raise your children to be civil, and to make a clear distinction between riches of character and those of a baser material.

Letter to Martha Washington from Philadelphia on learning of his appointment as commander in chief of the American forces, June 18, 1775: "SO FAR FROM SEEKING THIS APPOINTMENT I HAVE USED EVERY ENDEAVOR IN MY POWER TO AVOID IT . . . IT BEING TOO GREAT A TRUST FOR MY CAPACITY."

BREAK NOT A JEST WHERE NONE TAKE PLEASURE IN MIRTH; LAUGH NOT ALOUD NOR AT ALL WITHOUT OCCASION; DERIDE NO MAN'S MISFORTUNE THOUGH THERE SEEM TO BE SOME CAUSE.

Be not a clown! There is a time to laugh—but not when another is crying because of a fall or hard luck (even if it is self-induced). Timing is everything; don't joke when those around you are not in a jocular mood. Excessive and inappropriate laughter is an unfeeling and uncivil display.

SPEAK NOT INJURIOUS WORDS, NEITHER IN JEST NOR IN EARNEST; SCOFF AT NONE ALTHOUGH THEY GIVE OCCASION.

Even as children playing with sticks and stones, we knew (contrary to our responsive taunt) that words *can* hurt us. Be an adult. Do not hurl hateful verbal barbs at anyone (particularly children); they belie your maturity and confirm your incivility. A joke at another's expense is a nasty deed.

A SHORT TALE OF CIVILITY

Restoring Self-Composure

Everyone had assembled for the house closing—the buyers, the sellers, the real estate agents, and the settlement attorney who would conduct the affairs of the day—and everyone was a bit anxious.

In the middle of the proceedings, the seller became agitated and, without saying why, rolled up a piece of paper and threw it in the direction of her agent. The room itself seemed in shock. The settlement attorney turned to the woman. Politely and in a soft voice, he told her that if she had an issue to discuss she should talk about it in a civil and businesslike manner. Silence. She took in his words, gathered herself together, and was able to go on to complete the sale.

A calm voice and a firm presence can bring responsible behavior back into a room.

Rule 66

BE NOT FORWARD [OBSTINATE] BUT
FRIENDLY AND COURTEOUS, THE FIRST
TO SALUTE, HEAR, AND ANSWER.
BE NOT PENSIVE WHEN IT'S A TIME
TO CONVERSE.

Few of us are accused of being too friendly. The civil person puts others at ease by smiling, initiates friendly conversation, engages people, and is responsive. Standing stiffly on ceremony can be an impediment. But what of those awkward moments—on the plane, in the airport shuttle, on the bus? A greeting and a smile are always in order, but start a conversation with a seatmate only if it seems welcome.

The time for thinking about a matter should be followed by an expression of those thoughts. Silence might be mistaken for an expression you did not intend (disapproval, for instance). Speak up after you've thought through an issue.

DETRACT NOT FROM OTHERS, NEITHER BE EXCESSIVE IN COMMANDING.

A civil person does not disparage, decry, or belittle but gives others their due and affords them their say. Respect your colleagues' style and approach as you would have them respect yours. To be an ensemble player on the stage of life, avoid hogging the spotlight. Although it is easy to see yourself as the star of the show, remember that life is not a soliloquy.

A SHORT TALE OF CIVILITY

Demanding Service

On what would ordinarily be a leisurely afternoon, I agreed to accompany my wife to the mall because the store we would be going to had extremely courteous and helpful employees.

The men's shoe department, which had a tremendous selection and knowledgeable salespeople, was having its semiannual sale. My wife excused herself to go to the rest room. It was very busy and I was politely asked to take a seat until someone was free to help me. I looked around at the great variety of shoes as I waited my turn. Several salespeople were moving very quickly with boxes of shoes stacked in their arms.

Suddenly a man sitting in my row raised his voice and yelled in the direction of a passing sales clerk, "I have been here for fifteen minutes and no one has waited on me yet!" The salesman stopped in his tracks and replied in a very polite tone, "We are trying, sir. I will be with you as soon as I possibly can," to which the man retorted very loudly, "I want service!"

When the salesman leaned over to speak to me, I offered to come back at another time. "No," he said. "I will take care of you." Then I raised my voice. "You have to deal with that complainer." I glanced in the direction of the loud, rude man.

Next the man was towering over me. I stood up so that we were face to face. There were several moments of silence. Looking him in the eye, I asked in a calm voice, "What are you going to do now?" He thought it over: Then, in a mild voice, he said, "Nothing," returned to his seat, and waited his turn.

Although the salesman could not challenge the impatient and demanding customer, I could. Someone had to let him know he had crossed the line of civility. My wife returned. Believe it or not, she liked the pair of shoes I had chosen.

GO NOT THITHER, WHERE YOU KNOW NOT WHETHER YOU SHALL BE WELCOME. GIVE NOT ADVICE WITHOUT BEING ASKED AND, WHEN DESIRED, DO SO BRIEFLY.

Gold-trimmed invitations and visiting cards are not the custom of our times, but even so you know when you are not welcome in a personal or social situation. Be sure your presence is desired before your foot crosses the threshold. Knowing if your advice is welcome is even trickier. Like most of us, you believe your wise counsel is prime and rare. Restrain from meddling, especially in family matters, unless your advice is asked for. Do not impose or offer your views—but you can, of course, say, "It seems to me . . . ," which is a gentle way of stating your opinion.

Rule 69

IF TWO CONTEND TOGETHER, TAKE NOT
THE PART OF EITHER UNCONSTRAINED
AND BE NOT OBSTINATE IN YOUR OWN
OPINION. IN THINGS INDIFFERENT BE
OF THE MAJOR SIDE.

Perception varies with the view. Remember that another set of eyes has a different perspective. Your view is only one of many; a landscape seen through a telescope, kaleidoscope, or microscope assumes a unique aspect. Honor a friend by respecting that friend's opinion even though it differs from yours. If the issue is of little importance, let it go. How important is it to be "right"?

REPREHEND NOT THE IMPERFECTIONS OF OTHERS, FOR THAT BELONGS TO PARENTS, MASTERS, AND SUPERIORS.

Who are we to judge others? Leave judgment to those in charge. Empathize, don't criticize. As a boss or co-worker, as a friend, and as a parent, couch your censure as well-intentioned constructive criticism. You have arrived as a civil person when you are no longer judgmental.

GAZE NOT ON THE MARKS OR BLEMISHES OF OTHERS AND ASK NOT HOW THEY CAME. WHAT YOU MAY SPEAK IN SECRET TO YOUR FRIEND DELIVER NOT BEFORE OTHERS.

Control your curiosity and hold your tongue when you meet people with disfiguring marks. Do not avert your eyes and do not stare—both of which make a person self-conscious. If you apply the golden rule, you will always be discreet with your comments.

SPEAK NOT IN AN UNKNOWN TONGUE IN COMPANY BUT IN YOUR OWN LANGUAGE, AND THAT AS THOSE OF QUALITY DO AND NOT AS THE VULGAR. SUBLIME MATTERS TREAT SERIOUSLY.

Those who use a foreign language in the company of people who don't speak that language are like children employing exclusionary tactics. I'm sure you've felt left out in such a situation. Don't subject others to the same emotion. It is rude to carry on a conversation in a tongue that is not known to all present. Foul language has become much more common than it was in George's time; nevertheless, it remains uncivil and vulgar. As GW further urges us, be of a serious mood in dealing with matters of import.

Rule 73

THINK BEFORE YOU SPEAK, PRONOUNCE
NOT IMPERFECTLY, NOR BRING OUT
YOUR WORDS TOO HASTILY, BUT
ORDERLY AND DISTINCTLY.

Sift your thoughts before serving them up; the dish will be far tastier to those who consume it. Measure your phrases carefully, so they do not flood the ears of those who receive them. Thinking and listening before speaking applies to family, social, and business situations. You need not abandon spontaneity and sincerity. It takes only a moment to weigh the mode of the message as well as the message itself. As you perfect the process, you add the finishing touch—a layer of consideration and empathy— to all you say.

Organize your thoughts before you open your mouth. What comes out should be a clear and logical expression of the workings of a fine and logical brain. And deliver the goods with clarity; mumbling and stumbling will not do the job.

WHEN ANOTHER SPEAKS, BE ATTENTIVE YOURSELF AND DISTURB NOT THE AUDIENCE. IF ANY HESITATE IN HIS WORDS, HELP HIM NOT NOR PROMPT HIM WITHOUT BEING ASKED. INTERRUPT HIM NOT, NOR ANSWER HIM TILL HIS SPEECH BE ENDED.

Listening 101 should be a required course in all stages of our education, beginning with preschool. As we advance from one grade to the next, we would learn to be attentive, to wait for the speaker to finish, and to refrain from interrupting and blurting out a thought we fear we will not remember. Advanced students would be able to wait until a question is finished before beginning to answer it—just in case the question did not end the way they thought it would.

All good interviewers (holders of graduate degrees in Listening 101) hear people out and wait patiently for their turn to speak. They demonstrate courtesy and civility. And they learn a great deal from listening carefully.

In the *Courtroom*

In the courtroom, the defense attorney is cross-examining the witness against his client, the defendant, whom he believes has been falsely accused of robbery. The witness, confused about who might have committed the crime, slowly begins to crumble under the questioning. Tears well up in her eyes and stream down her cheeks.

The adversary, the defense lawyer, is about to ask her another tough question. Instead, he pauses, approaches her . . . and hands her several tissues.

We are all human beings. Even a lawyer during a critical moment in an important trial does not have to be unfeeling and uncivil.

Rule 75

IN THE MIDST OF DISCOURSE ASK NOT
OF WHAT ONE TREATS, BUT IF YOU
PERCEIVE ANY TO STOP BECAUSE OF
YOUR COMING YOU MAY WELL
ENTREAT HIM TO PROCEED. IF A
PERSON OF QUALITY COMES IN WHILE
YOU ARE CONVERSING, IT IS HANDSOME
TO REPEAT WHAT WAS SAID BEFORE.

We've all experienced those mildly uncomfortable moments when someone joins a group immersed in conversation. You should not expect a recap if you come into the middle of a conversation. However, you may extend this courtesy to someone who arrives later. The best solution may be to present a summary of what has transpired.

WHILE YOU ARE TALKING, POINT NOT
WITH YOUR FINGER AT HIM OF WHOM
YOU DISCOURSE, NOR APPROACH TOO
NEAR TO HIM TO WHOM YOU TALK,
ESPECIALLY TO HIS FACE.

"Get your finger out of my face!" As sad as it is to utter those words, imagine how rude the person is who provokes them. Physical proximity can be threatening. You should keep a proper distance when conversing with another—unless that person is a lover, coach, or umpire.

TREAT WITH MEN AT FIT TIMES ABOUT BUSINESS AND WHISPER NOT IN THE COMPANY OF OTHERS.

Your business may be all-important to you—and to some of those around you. But know when and to whom it is of little interest, and do not stir it into every conversation and situation. Be sure your companion finds matters of commerce and industry suitable topics for the occasion.

Plain and simple: Whispering is an act of rudeness—an affront to those in your company. If you cannot speak the words to all present, stifle yourself!

MAKE NO COMPARISONS, AND IF ANY OF THE COMPANY BE COMMENDED FOR ANY BRAVE ACT OF VIRTUE, COMMEND NOT ANOTHER FOR THE SAME.

Comparisons, except for sales figures, are usually a poor idea. Never, ever, compare your children—to one another or to others. Comparing people is a bad idea that leads to no good. Comparing actions is equally unwise. An act of virtue or bravery should be singled out as special.

BE NOT APT TO RELATE NEWS IF YOU
KNOW NOT THE TRUTH THEREOF.
IN DISCOURSING OF THINGS YOU HAVE
HEARD, NAME NOT YOUR AUTHOR.
ALWAYS A SECRET DISCOVER NOT.

Rumormongering, like gossiping, is a most uncivil enterprise. Verify the "news" before you spread it, or, like the seed of the nastiest weed, it will take root and sprout. If you are privy to information of a sensitive nature, shield your source and be discreet in broadcasting it. Sound judgment in such matters is as central to success in the next century as it was in the previous one. George's final admonishment is to keep your nose out of another's tent. In other words, don't pry.

BE NOT TEDIOUS IN DISCOURSE OR IN READING UNLESS YOU FIND THE COMPANY PLEASED THEREWITH.

The long graduation speech bores us as it would have bored GW. Verbosity should be a misdemeanor. Discuss a matter crisply, and exercise your sense of empathy to be sure you are not boring people.

A SHORT TALE OF CIVILITY
When Less Is More

Each year a business professor I know announces to his class that a point that cannot be made in five minutes or less is not worth making. His students often chuckle at the irony that a college professor, notorious drones that they are, makes this claim. Amazingly enough, he doggedly abides by this principle. He never speaks for more than five minutes on a particular topic. He is a genius at getting students to participate and share their own experiences. It is not unusual for him to challenge a student to lead the entire class on a particular topic. In short, he teaches by example.

BE NOT CURIOUS TO KNOW THE AFFAIRS OF OTHERS, NEITHER APPROACH THOSE THAT SPEAK IN PRIVATE.

Tending to your own life is a full-time job; sometimes it goes into overtime! How in the world do people find time to intrude on the lives of others? In our more civil society, there will be no room for nosy people or for those who horn in on private conversations.

UNDERTAKE NOT WHAT YOU CANNOT PERFORM BUT BE CAREFUL TO KEEP YOUR PROMISE.

Resist the urge to accept the pass when you know you cannot make it to the goal line. When we overcommit ourselves, we are likely to become anxious and fumble the ball. If you know you cannot score, say no. It is far better to refuse the handoff than to disappoint the team and lose the game. An exhausted player needs to sit out a quarter despite the urge to keep going.

A promise is to keep. Trust is based on performing on your promises. You should always be there when it counts. People rely on you, and you should be willing to make a personal sacrifice to meet your commitments.

When the peace treaty with Great Britain was finally signed, ending the American Revolution, George Washington was fifty-one years old. Having made the commitment to command the troops, he had been in uniform more than eight years. During that entire period, he had spent only three days at his Mount Vernon home. To keep a promise, George Washington believed in sacrifice—he lost half his net worth during the Revolutionary War.

Rule 83

WHEN YOU DELIVER A MATTER [MESSAGE], DO IT WITHOUT PASSION AND WITH DISCRETION HOWEVER MEAN THE PERSON YOU DO IT TO.

Be like the mail carrier: Transmit the package with a professional air. Say nothing, don't raise your eyebrows, and don't sneer.

Rule 84

WHEN YOUR SUPERIORS TALK TO ANYBODY, HEARKEN NOT, NEITHER SPEAK NOR LAUGH.

Eavesdropping—by intent or accident—is a form of theft. Snoops and spies are not welcome in most businesses, so don't listen to words not meant for you. Avoid interrupting those in conversation, especially the boss. Develop a professional attitude if you wish to get ahead.

IN THE COMPANY OF THOSE OF HIGHER
QUALITY THAN YOURSELF, SPEAK NOT
TILL YOU ARE ASKED A QUESTION,
THEN STAND UPRIGHT, PUT OFF YOUR
HAT, AND ANSWER IN A FEW WORDS.

Times and manners change, and so do we. Although today we are all of the same quality and do not need to wait until spoken to (and need not wear a hat), we can afford the questioner the pleasure of a brief response.

Rule 86

IN DISPUTE BE NOT SO DESIROUS TO
OVERCOME AS NOT TO GIVE LIBERTY TO
EACH ONE TO DELIVER HIS OPINION AND
SUBMIT TO THE JUDGMENT OF THE
MAJOR PART, ESPECIALLY IF THEY
ARE JUDGES OF THE DISPUTE.

How tempting it is to raise our voice and overwhelm others in a dispute, but consensus is still the best way to settle a controversy. Think of the early days of our republic and of the many signatures on the Declaration of Independence. Remember the Founding Fathers' emphasis on the collective intelligence. Follow their example and wisdom in gathering the facts, weighing the possibilities, and asking others for their opinions as you engage in a decision-making process. As we advance, we should also look back; the tools of arbitration and mediation give us a civil way to resolve disputes.

LET YOUR CARRIAGE BE SUCH AS
BECOMES A MAN: GRAVE, SETTLED,
AND ATTENTIVE TO THAT WHICH IS
SPOKEN. CONTRADICT NOT AT EVERY
TURN WHAT OTHERS SAY.

The word "carriage"—deportment—comes from a bygone era. Webster's, in fact, calls it archaic. What a shame. A person's carriage tells us much. A grave, settled, and attentive person shows respect to those present, pays mind to what is being said, and does not arbitrarily contradict others. We would all do well to note our carriage now and then.

BE NOT TEDIOUS IN DISCOURSE, MAKE NOT MANY DIGRESSIONS, NOR REPEAT OFTEN THE SAME MANNER OF DISCOURSE.

Repeat after me: I will not repeat myself. I will not repeat myself. I will not . . .

You get the point: Redundancy is an annoyance. And the tedious speaker runs the risk of losing the audience. So when you speak, stick to the point, spice up your vocabulary, and enthrall your listeners.

SPEAK NOT EVIL OF THE ABSENT, FOR IT IS UNJUST.

Fairness is basic to our entire social system. Never speak ill of someone who is not present to mount a defense or to set the record straight. If ever there was a golden opportunity to exercise the golden rule, this is it.

BEING SET AT MEAT, SCRATCH NOT, NEITHER SPIT, COUGH, NOR BLOW YOUR NOSE EXCEPT WHEN THERE'S A NECESSITY FOR IT.

This one is child's play, or should be. Good table manners (always in order) should be second nature rather than a rule of behavior. When at table, imagine a mirror before you and ask yourself if you would like to be the person sitting opposite. As in all matters of behavior, knowledge and execution are both important.

MAKE NO SHOW OF TAKING GREAT
DELIGHT IN YOUR VICTUALS. FEED NOT
WITH GREEDINESS. EAT YOUR BREAD
WITH A KNIFE, LEAN NOT ON THE
TABLE, NEITHER FIND FAULT WITH
WHAT YOU EAT.

Relish your relish—but not to extremes. And don't gulp your meal in one . . .gulp. A piecemeal approach (cutting your food into small bits) can spread out the spread, and everyone can enjoy the time at the table. Be grateful for sustenance and hold the complaints. As you converse and catch up with companions, you might light a candle; even old silver glows in its light.

Rule 92

TAKE NO SALT NOR CUT BREAD WITH YOUR KNIFE GREASY.

See how we have evolved! Still, today we must remember not to double-dip our chips.

ENTERTAINING ANYONE AT THE
TABLE, IT IS DECENT TO PRESENT HIM
WITH MEAT. UNDERTAKE NOT TO HELP
OTHERS UNDESIRED BY THE MASTER.

Vegetarian dinners are fine today, of course. What George is getting at is the importance of offering your guests the best you can afford. Do not serve your guests a meager meal. Be as generous as you are hospitable. (George's last comment in this rule refers to a less egalitarian time than ours.)

Rule 94

IF YOU SOAK BREAD IN THE SAUCE, LET
IT BE NO MORE THAN WHAT YOU PUT IN
YOUR MOUTH AT A TIME, AND BLOW
NOT YOUR BROTH AT THE TABLE BUT
STAY TILL IT COOLS OF ITSELF.

Don't stuff, don't puff, and don't huff. Slurping should be reserved for the frozen confection.

Rule 95

PUT NOT YOUR MEAT TO YOUR MOUTH
WITH YOUR KNIFE IN YOUR HAND;
NEITHER SPIT FORTH THE STONES OF
ANY FRUIT PIE NOR CAST ANYTHING
UNDER THE TABLE.

Cut with your knife but eat with your fork, the preferred utensil for delivering food to the mouth. Spitting (except on the baseball field and in the hockey rink) is still frowned upon. Throwing anything under the table—even if the dog catches it on the fly—shows poor breeding.

IT IS UNBECOMING TO STOOP MUCH TO
ONE'S MEAT. KEEP YOUR FINGERS
CLEAN AND, WHEN FOUL, WIPE THEM
ON A CORNER OF YOUR TABLE NAPKIN.

It is folly to bend over when with the same expenditure of energy your food can be brought to your mouth. Lift your fork and spoon! Although the days of finger bowls are past, the need for clean fingers at the table is not. Use your napkin, not the tablecloth or your clothes.

Rule 97

PUT NOT ANOTHER BITE INTO YOUR MOUTH TILL THE FORMER BE SWALLOWED. LET NOT YOUR MORSELS BE TOO BIG FOR THE JOWLS.

Don't wolf down your food—even if you are dining with Little Red Riding Hood's grandmother. Your stomach will more easily digest the food that you have chewed. Even a mighty hungry beast should spare dining companions the view of an unsightly stuffed mouth. A glutton is never a welcome guest.

DRINK NOT NOR TALK WITH YOUR MOUTH FULL, NEITHER GAZE ABOUT YOU WHILE YOU ARE DRINKING.

At the very least, consider the possibility of choking while trying to talk as you eat and drink. This rule, which has been with us for at least 250 years, protects us against more than the charge of poor manners. Your companions may not be skilled in CPR. You may, however, look around as you drink unless your aim is affected, causing a slip between the cup and your lip.

DRINK NOT TOO LEISURELY NOR YET
TOO HASTILY. BEFORE AND AFTER
DRINKING, WIPE YOUR LIPS. BREATHE
NOT THEN OR EVER WITH TOO GREAT
NOISE, FOR IT IS UNCIVIL.

Drink it up or drink it down but time it right. Do not slurp—and be neat to save on laundry bills. As you imbibe your beverage (and at other times), breathe softly and quietly. Loud breathing is like loud talking. There is never a good reason for it except in an emergency.

CLEANSE NOT YOUR TEETH WITH THE TABLECLOTH, NAPKIN, FORK, OR KNIFE, BUT IF OTHERS DO IT, LET IT BE DONE WITH A TOOTHPICK.

Toothpicks may have been the tool of choice in George's day, but today using even color-coordinated ones to clean your teeth in public is considered a bit crude. Wait until you're in private and whip out your favorite dental floss, remembering to floss only those teeth you want to keep.

Rule 101

RINSE NOT YOUR MOUTH IN THE PRESENCE OF OTHERS.

Some acts should only be done in private.

Rule 102

IT IS OUT OF USE TO CALL UPON THE
COMPANY OFTEN TO EAT. NOR NEED
YOU DRINK TO OTHERS EVERY TIME
YOU DRINK.

Breaking bread has long forged the bonds of friendship, but it isn't necessary to eat and drink every time you get together with friends. Lift your glass in toast once only, save the calories, and suggest a walk.

Rule 103

In the company of your betters, be not longer in eating than they are. Lay not your arm but only your hand upon the table.

It's nice to keep pace with your dining companions (whoever they are)—and if you are able, keep those elbows (and arms) off the table.

IT BELONGS TO THE CHIEFEST IN THE
COMPANY TO UNFOLD HIS NAPKIN AND
FALL TO MEAT FIRST. BUT HE OUGHT
THEN TO BEGIN IN TIME AND TO
DISPATCH WITH DEXTERITY, THAT
THE SLOWEST MAY HAVE TIME
ALLOWED HIM.

As tempting the smells, as hungry the stomach, the
mannered guest awaits the host to begin the meal. The
host, in turn, tries not the patience of the guests—for
someday the tables may be turned.

Rule 105

BE NOT ANGRY AT THE TABLE, WHATEVER HAPPENS, AND IF YOU HAVE REASON TO BE SO, SHOW IT NOT BUT PUT ON A CHEERFUL COUNTENANCE, ESPECIALLY IF THERE BE A STRANGER, FOR GOOD HUMOR MAKES ONE DISH OF MEAT A FEAST.

A scowl is inappropriate garb at the table. Even in your finest clothes, you'll make a very poor impression. Put on a happy face and muster up high spirits. A happy band of diners enhances the finest meal.

Rule 106

SET NOT YOURSELF AT THE UPPER SIDE
OF THE TABLE, BUT IF IT BE YOUR DUE
OR THAT THE MASTER OF THE HOUSE
WILL HAVE IT SO. CONTEND NOT, LEST
YOU SHOULD TROUBLE THE COMPANY.

A place for everything and everyone: The well-
mannered guest does not sit in the host's seat unless asked
to do so. Nor does a guest argue about such matters.

Rule 107

IF OTHERS TALK AT THE TABLE, BE ATTENTIVE, BUT TALK NOT WITH MEAT IN YOUR MOUTH.

Talking with your mouth full was either a very serious transgression or GW's pet peeve. Like number 98, this rule (which applies to fish and poultry as well) focuses on a most distasteful practice. As we have noted, aside from the risk of choking, it is just plain bad manners. Concentrate on the conversation rather than on concentrating the food in your mouth.

WHEN YOU SPEAK OF GOD OR HIS
ATTRIBUTES, LET IT BE SERIOUSLY AND
WITH REVERENCE. HONOR AND OBEY
YOUR NATURAL PARENTS, THOUGH
THEY BE POOR.

Respect religion and the guidelines it has provided for decency, civility, and good character. Although one can be civilized without being religious, formalized religions and religious teachings have spurred many to do great things.

Honoring your parents, Commandment Five, may be difficult when you have differences of opinion with them, but those differences and issues of wealth should not be the source of dishonorable treatment. Teenagers are sometimes inclined to snarl and snap at their parents most disrespectfully for a period of years, but most come through those difficult times to finally appreciate the guidance their parents gave them.

LET YOUR RECREATIONS BE MANFUL, NOT SINFUL.

If only every man (and woman) could live by this rule. . . .

A SHORT TALE OF CIVILITY

Road Rage

The situation on our highways may be the most common form of incivility we encounter these days. As more and more people try to drive on roads that were not meant to carry the current load, traffic conditions get worse and worse. Drivers become frustrated by delays and tempers flare.

Of course, we ought to be extending courtesies to those who share the road with us. Why not let someone into your lane? You would take the time and expend the effort to hold a door open for someone entering your office building. Perhaps we all need to let go of the selfishness that seems to take over when we get behind the wheel.

If you witness an aggressive driver on the road and you have a phone in your car, you can do something about the menace. Virtually all states have made stopping aggressive drivers a priority. Signs on many highways give a phone number you can call to report a dangerous and inconsiderate driver. Drunk drivers should certainly be reported as soon as possible. Calling the police is a better solution than countering with your own aggression, which may be dangerous for you and for those in your car, as well as for others who happen to be traveling the same road. Take a stand for civility on the highway. Drive in a responsible manner and report those who do not.

Rule 110

LABOR TO KEEP ALIVE IN YOUR BREAST THAT LITTLE SPARK OF CELESTIAL FIRE CALLED CONSCIENCE.

For his final rule, George points us in the direction of the source of all rules: our conscience, which he refers to as a spark that must be kept alive. If your fire is extinguished, your compass is gone and you will lose your way on the trail of life. Stoke the coals and send up a bright flame that others may see and follow.

A SHORT TALE OF CIVILITY

At the Gym

Even the most casual exchange and simple act of civility can enhance your life. A woman who was working out at her gym asked the desk attendant for aspirin. He said they had just run out. A man within earshot offered to go out to his car to get some. Despite her protests that the weather was wintry, this gentleman jogged out to his car in his shorts and T-shirt and returned with a small bottle of pills. The grateful woman thanked him.

Months later, the woman saw the man's picture in the paper with a notice that he was giving a talk about a book he had written. She and her daughter attended the event and joined in a lively discussion, and in the months that followed a fine friendship was formed. A gesture of civility in the form of an aspirin had enriched the lives of three people.

From a letter to Joseph Reed, January 14, 1776: "FOR AS I HAVE BUT ONE CAPITAL OBJECT IN VIEW, I COULD WISH TO MAKE MY CONDUCT COINCIDE WITH THE WISHES OF MANKIND AS FAR AS I CAN CONSISTENTLY."

TEN OTHER CIVIL THINGS
YOU CAN DO

Treating others with a high degree of civility goes hand in hand with your own positive feelings toward life. These ten suggestions, which supplement George's rules, may help bring you a greater sense of being plugged into life.

1. ***Think of yourself as a human being first.*** Most people identify themselves in terms of their jobs or what they do: dentist, lawyer, carpenter, teacher, computer analyst, mother, homemaker, teacher, and so on. Try thinking of yourself as a person first who just happens to work in a certain area. If you view yourself in this way, you are likely to develop a stronger sense of empathy with other people. Remember the strain of common humanity that runs through all of us and the capacity we have to find it in each other.

2. ***Be tolerant of other people.*** At the very foundation of a civil society is tolerance. Being tolerant sounds easy, but it takes effort. Work on your ability to allow for

differences in the way other people perceive the world, speak, and act.

3. ***Attend family gatherings.*** Your family is a constant in your life that provides lifelong identity and a sense of self and security. When you stay in touch with your family, you maintain bonds with people who stabilize your life.

4. ***Stay abreast of the news.*** Keep in touch with events and politics in your neighborhood, your region, your state, your country, and the world. A sense of community is one of the building blocks of a civil world. Read newspapers and news magazines, turn on radio and television news, and attend meetings to keep informed.

5. ***Join a civic organization.*** To connect to those in your immediate community, lend your efforts to a civic organization. You will join people who are involved in furthering the common good through charitable undertakings. Participants in civic organizations get acquainted under the best of circumstances: a joint effort to improve the community.

6. ***Take up gardening.*** Being in touch with nature is very satisfying. As you dig and till the soil and encourage plants to produce nature's bounty, you feel in harmony with the earth. Your appreciation of the change of seasons and the weather, of the rain and the sun, and of the interdependence of all living things is heightened. It is much like sensitivity training.

7. ***Participate in a team sport.*** Choose a sport and a level of play that suits you. In addition to developing a sense of camaraderie with your team members, you will make enduring friendships that go beyond game time. A team that imparts good values, a spirit of trying, good sportsmanship, and healthy exercise can give you a new outlook on life.

8. ***Dance.*** Every dance form can give you an enhanced feeling of life. You connect with others when you move in rhythm to music. Dancing with a single partner or joining a group in a line or circle dance gives you a unique feeling of being alive. (If you don't know how, learn!)

9. ***Volunteer.*** By giving time, effort, or possessions to helping others, we help ourselves. Recognize the ways in which you can contribute to the lives of fellow human beings, be it in a homeless shelter, a school or camp, or other organized effort. You will find those activities are as meaningful to you as to those you help.

10. ***Protect the environment.*** As you work to improve the environment, you bring yourself closer to the human community. An appreciation of life should include respect for the earth. Join in conservation efforts and your town's recycling endeavors. Be environmentally aware.

A LAST WORD

Civility starts with you. As you work toward practices of greater courtesy and consideration, see how your life improves. Watch the effects expand and touch the lives of others. Just as a stone thrown into a pool of still water creates ripples in ever-spreading concentric circles, so does the practice of civility affect society. But like those watery ripples, the effect dies down unless the effort continues.

Civility is a precious resource. Use it and recycle it.

KEY DATES IN THE LIFE OF
GEORGE WASHINGTON

1732   Washington was born February 22 in Westmore-land Country, Virginia.

1746   At fourteen, he wrote down 110 rules under the title "Rules of Civility and Decent Behavior in Company and Conversation."

1749   He was appointed surveyor for Culpeper County, Virginia.

1753   Governor Robert Dinwiddie sent him to the Ohio Valley to warn the French that they were en-croaching on British territory, an admonition they ignored.

1754   Promoted to lieutenant colonel, Washington was dispatched to a fort where Pittsburgh now stands to help guard it against the French, who defeated him at Great Meadows, Pennsylvania.

1755   After resigning his commission and returning to farming in 1754, he was chosen to join the staff of British general Edward Braddock during the

French and Indian War; at Fort Duquesne he fought bravely but unsuccessfully against the Indians.

1755 Returned unhurt to his Mount Vernon home, he was shortly made commander in chief of the Virginia militia by the governor.

1758 Leading a successful campaign against the French as they retreated, he then retired from the army.

1759 Washington married Martha Dandridge Custis, a young widow, managed their properties and served in the Virginia legislature, the House of Burgesses.

1774 He was a delegate to the First Continental Congress in Philadelphia.

1775 Sent as delegate to the Second Continental Congress, he was unanimously elected commander in chief of the American forces.

1783 After leading his troops successfully in the Revolutionary War, he retired to Mount Vernon.

1787 Washington came out of retirement to attend and preside over the federal convention at which thirty-nine delegates from twelve states signed the Constitution.

1789 He was unanimously elected first president of the United States.

1793 Without opposition, he served a second term as U.S. president.